Vocal Selections

OKLAHOMA!

*A Rodgers & Hammerstein
Commemorative Edition*

The first United States postage stamp honoring a Broadway Musical. Issued nationwide March 31, 1993

*Rodgers and Hammerstein and the R&H logo are trademarks used under license from The Rodgers and Hammerstein Organization
on behalf of the Rodgers Family Partnership and the Estate of Oscar Hammerstein II.*

*The Sound Of Music is a registered trademark used under license from The Rodgers and Hammerstein Organization on behalf of the Rodgers Family Partnership,
the Estate of Oscar Hammerstein II and the heirs of Howard Lindsay and Russel Crouse.*

Williamson Music is a registered trademark of the Rodgers Family Partnership and the Estate of Oscar Hammerstein II.

ISBN 0-7395-1861-X

WILLIAMSON MUSIC®
A RODGERS AND HAMMERSTEIN COMPANY

EXCLUSIVELY DISTRIBUTED BY

HAL•LEONARD®
CORPORATION
7777 W. BLUEMOUND RD. P.O. BOX 13819 MILWAUKEE, WI 53213

A Rodgers & Hammerstein Commemorative Edition

OKLAHOMA!™

Contents

Backdrop for Act II, Scene 1, by Lemuel Ayres from the original 1943 production

PHOTOS, CLOCKWISE FROM
UPPER LEFT:
Oscar Hammerstein II and
Richard Rodgers in rehearsals,
spring 1943.

•

Alfred Drake (Curly) and Joan
Roberts (Laurey).

•

Celeste Holm (Ado Annie) and
Lee Dixon (Will Parker).

TOP: Surrounding the surrey, from left to right: Lee Dixon (Will Parker), Celeste Holm (Ado Annie), Alfred Drake (Curly), Joan Roberts (Laurey), Joseph Buloff (Ali Hakim) and Betty Garde (Aunt Eller) with members of the company in the finale.

•

CENTER: Jud Fry's "postcard girls" are brought to life in the "Dream Ballet." From left to right: Joan McCracken, Kate Friedlich, Margit DeKova, Bobby Barentine and Vivian Smith.

•

BOTTOM RIGHT: "Pore Jud Is Daid"; Howard da Silva (Jud) and Alfred Drake (Curly).

TOP LEFT: Poster from the

original release.

•

TOP RIGHT: Gene Nelson (Will

Parker) shows off a rope trick

he learned in "Kansas City".

CENTER RIGHT: Shirley Jones

as Laurey.

•

BOTTOM RIGHT: "Oh, What A

Beautiful Mornin'", Gordon MacRae

as Curly.

ON LOCATION IN NOGALES,

ARIZONA, SUMMER 1954.

ABOVE: Hammerstein confers with

director Fred Zinneman.

•

BELOW: Gene Nelson (Will Parker)

chats with Richard Rodgers

between takes.

TOP LEFT: Poster from the 1979 Broadway revival

•

BOTTOM, CLOCKWISE FROM LEFT: Dream Laurey (Louise Hickey) reacts in horror to a moment in the climactic "Dream Ballet".

•

Mary Wickes (Aunt Eller) and Laurence Guittard (Curly).

•

Harry Groener (Will Parker) kicks up his heels in "Kansas City".

•

Laurence Guittard (Curly) lulls Christine Andreas (Laurey) with his description of "The Surrey With The Fringe On Top".

© 1979 Martha Swope

The quintessentially American spirit of *OKLAHOMA!* has, paradoxically, made it an endearing and enduring popular favorite worldwide. It has been translated into over a dozen languages and presented in hundreds of productions across the globe. Among the more unusual: an all-female cast presented by Japan's famed Takarazuka Company (1967), and another, performed nightly, on a ferry shuttling between Helsinki and Stockholm (1993).

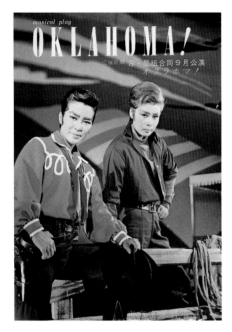

Takarazuka Theatre, Tokyo, Japan (1967)

Theater des Westens, Berlin, West Germany (1982)

Sheet music from the film (France)

Poster for the film (Poland)

Oslo Nye Theater, Norway (1988)

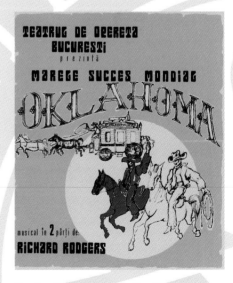

Teatrug de Opereta, Bucharest, Rumania

OKLAHOMA!

Time Line

JANUARY 26, 1931 – The Theatre Guild presents Lynn Riggs' play GREEN GROW THE LILACS on Broadway, where it runs for 64 performances...A native of Oklahoma, Riggs drew from his childhood memories of the Indian Territory's transformation into statehood for the historical context within his play.

JULY 23, 1942 – THE NEW YORK TIMES reports: "The Theatre Guild announced yesterday that Richard Rodgers, Lorenz Hart and Oscar Hammerstein II will soon begin work on a musical version of Lynn Riggs' folk-play GREEN GROW THE LILACS." Shortly thereafter lyricist Hart drops out of the project and Hammerstein takes over his duties. The resulting musical is the first in the Rodgers & Hammerstein collaboration, which goes on to yield such classics as CAROUSEL, SOUTH PACIFIC, THE KING AND I and THE SOUND OF MUSIC.

MARCH 11-13, 1943 – The new musical has its world premiere engagement at the Shubert Theatre, New Haven. Entitled AWAY WE GO!, the work is termed "a musical play" with book and lyrics by Oscar Hammerstein II, based on the play GREEN GROW THE LILACS by Lynn Riggs, with music by Richard Rodgers. Presented by The Theatre Guild, it is directed by Rouben Mamoulian, choreographed by Agnes de Mille, settings designed by Lemuel Ayers and costumes by Miles White. The company includes Alfred Drake (Curly), Joan Roberts (Laurey), Betty Garde (Aunt Eller), Lee Dixon (Will Parker) and Celeste Holm (Ado Annie.)

MARCH 15-27, 1943 – AWAY WE GO! plays the Colonial Theatre, Boston, where changes are made prior to the show's Broadway premiere. One song is cut, "Boys And Girls Like You And Me." A second act choral number, originally slated as a duet for Curly and Laurey, is introduced during the wedding scene late in Act II. Entitled "Oklahoma," it stops the show.

MARCH 31, 1943 – With an exclamation point tacked on for extra flourish, the Act II showstopper becomes the musical's title song when OKLAHOMA! opens at the St. James Theatre on Broadway to rave reviews...On **December 2, 1943** Decca Records releases the original Broadway cast recording of OKLAHOMA!, marking the first time a musical is recorded complete with all members of the original cast, chorus and orchestra; the album eventually earns a Gold Record and in 1976 is inducted into the NARAS (Grammy Award) Hall of Fame...On **May 2, 1944** OKLAHOMA! receives a special Pulitzer Prize for Drama...On **July 1, 1946**, it surpasses HELLZAPOPPIN's run of 1404 performances to become the longest running musical in Broadway history...On **December 4, 1947**, with Richard Rodgers conducting the second act, it gives its 2000th performance on Broadway...On **May 29, 1948** it closes on Broadway after a marathon 2,212 performances — a Broadway record unsurpassed until MY FAIR LADY in 1961 — having been seen by more than 4 1/2 million people during the course of its five year engagement...On **May 31, 1948**, the Broadway company of OKLAHOMA! embarks upon a year long tour throughout the United States, visiting 67 cities.

OCTOBER 15, 1943 — The national tour of OKLAHOMA! opens at the Shubert Theatre, New Haven. It closes ten and a half years later at the Shubert Theatre, Philadelphia...During its decade-plus run, the touring company visits more than 250 cities encompassing every state in the Union before a total audience of 10,000,000...On **November 25, 1946** the tour gives its first performance in Oklahoma, and Governor Robert S. Kerr turns the event into a statewide celebration. Rodgers, Hammerstein, their wives and members of the musical's creative and production team attend the festivities, which include balls, parades, and culminate in eight sold-out performances of OKLAHOMA! in the Oklahoma City Municipal Auditorium...On **August 31, 1953**, less than five years after the musical has closed on Broadway, OKLAHOMA! returns to New York for a one week run at the New York City Center. With its arrival, OKLAHOMA! joins three other Rodgers & Hammerstein musicals already running on Broadway — SOUTH PACIFIC, THE KING AND I and ME AND JULIET — prompting Mayor Vincent R. Impelliteri to declare "Rodgers & Hammerstein Week."

FEBRUARY 26, 1945 — USO Camp Shows, Inc., under the supervision of Reginald and Ted Hammerstein (brother and cousin respectively to the librettist), launches a nine-month tour of OKLAHOMA! playing to the U.S. armed forces stationed in the Pacific theater.

APRIL 29, 1947 — OKLAHOMA! opens at the Theatre Royal, Drury Lane, London, with Harold (later Howard) Keel and Betty Jane Watson in the leading roles...Before it closes on **October 21, 1950**, OKLAHOMA! gives 1,548 performances in London, the longest run of any show in the 267 year history of the Drury Lane.

APRIL 28, 1953 — The Oklahoma State House of Representatives passes House Bill No. 1094,declaring the song "Oklahoma" by Richard Rodgers and Oscar Hammerstein II to be "the official song and anthem of the State of Oklahoma." The Senate ratifies the bill on **May 6, 1953**.

JUNE 20, 1955 — ANTA'S "Salute to France" presents OKLAHOMA! at the Theatre des Champs-Elysees, Paris. Jack Cassidy (Curly), Shirley Jones (Laurey) and Pamela Britton (Ado Annie) star in the production, which follows its Paris engagement with performances in Rome, Naples, Milan and Venice.

AUGUST 21, 1955 — Shirley Jones, Ed Sullivan, Eddie Fisher, Richard Rodgers, Oscar Hammerstein II and the governors of New York and Oklahoma lead an "OKLAHOMA! Song-Fest" at the Central Park Mall in New York before a crowd of 15,000.

OCTOBER 11, 1955 — The motion picture version of OKLAHOMA! is released. Presented by Rodgers & Hammerstein and directed by Fred Zinneman, it stars Gordon MacRae and Shirley Jones.

Time Line

JANUARY 10, 1968 – To celebrate the 25th Anniversary of the musical play OKLAHOMA! as well as the 60th anniversary of the state of Oklahoma, Governor Dewey F. Bartlett announces the formation of an honorary commission of nationally-recognized leaders in the public arts, the academic world and the business community to oversee events and commemorations pertaining to both anniversaries. Among those serving on the commission are: Ed Sullivan, Leonard Bernstein, Darryl Zanuck, Walter Cronkite, Johnny Carson, Fred Astaire, Mary Martin, Jack Benny, William Paley, Jackie Robinson, Perle Mesta, Chet Huntley, David Brinkley, Harry Belafonte, Art Buchwald, Maria Tallchief, Will Rogers, Jr., and Celeste Holm.

MARCH 26, 1968 – At Philharmonic (now Avery Fisher) Hall, Lincoln Center, in New York City, Skitch Henderson and Richard Rodgers conduct the New York Philharmonic Symphony Orchestra and an all-star cast in a Silver Anniversary concert version of OKLAHOMA! Staged by William Hammerstein, the evening features John Davidson (Curly), Constance Towers (Laurey), Anita Gillette (Ado Annie), Joseph Bova (Will Parker) and Margaret Hamilton (Aunt Eller.)

MAY 1, 1979 – A revival of OKLAHOMA! under the direction of William Hammerstein begins a cross-country national tour at the Pantages Theatre in Los Angeles...Tour sites include Washington D.C.'s Kennedy Center and Oklahoma City where, at the invitation of Governor George Nigh, OKLAHOMA! is presented in honor of the state's 72nd anniversary of statehood...On **December 13, 1979**, with Governor Nigh in attendance, this production opens at the Palace Theatre on Broadway, where it plays until **August 24, 1980** for a total of 293 performances, before going out on a post-Broadway national tour.

©1979 Martha Swope

OCTOBER 3, 1990 – Williamson Music Company, the music publishing subsidiary of Rodgers & Hammerstein, enters into an agreement with the state of Oklahoma, granting the state the right to use the song "Oklahoma" in the promotion of tourism. Waiving standard fees, Williamson Music charges the state of Oklahoma $1. The agreement is announced in Washington, D.C. by U.S. Senator David L. Boren of Oklahoma. Joining him for the announcement are Mary Rodgers, daughter of the composer, and William Hammerstein, son of the lyricist.

MARCH 31, 1993 – On the 50th anniversary of the Broadway premiere of OKLAHOMA!, the U.S. Postal Service issues a stamp commemorating the musical and the milestone. It is the first U.S. postage stamp honoring a Broadway musical.

TO DATE – Every year the Rodgers & Hammerstein Theatre Library licenses more than 600 productions of OKLAHOMA! in the United States and Canada alone. Worldwide, OKLAHOMA! has been presented throughout Great Britain, Australia and Japan as well as Berlin, Johannesburg, Stockholm, Oslo, Copenhagen, Rekjavik, Tel Aviv, Budapest, Belgrade, Paris and beyond.

OH, WHAT A BEAUTIFUL MORNIN'

Lyrics by OSCAR HAMMERSTEIN II
Music by RICHARD RODGERS

THE SURREY WITH THE FRINGE ON TOP

Lyrics by OSCAR HAMMERSTEIN II
Music by RICHARD RODGERS

KANSAS CITY

Lyrics by OSCAR HAMMERSTEIN I
Music by RICHARD RODGERS

I CAIN'T SAY NO!

Lyrics by OSCAR HAMMERSTEIN II
Music by RICHARD RODGERS

MANY A NEW DAY

Lyrics by OSCAR HAMMERSTEIN II
Music by RICHARD RODGERS

Why should a wom-an who is health - y and strong, blub-ber like a ba-by if her

man goes a - way? A - weep-in' and a - wail-in' how he done her wrong,

that's one thing you'll nev - er hear me say! Nev - er gon - na think that the

PEOPLE WILL SAY WE'RE IN LOVE

Lyrics by OSCAR HAMMERSTEIN II
Music by RICHARD RODGERS

41

PORE JUD IS DAID

Lyrics by OSCAR HAMMERSTEIN II
Music by RICHARD RODGERS

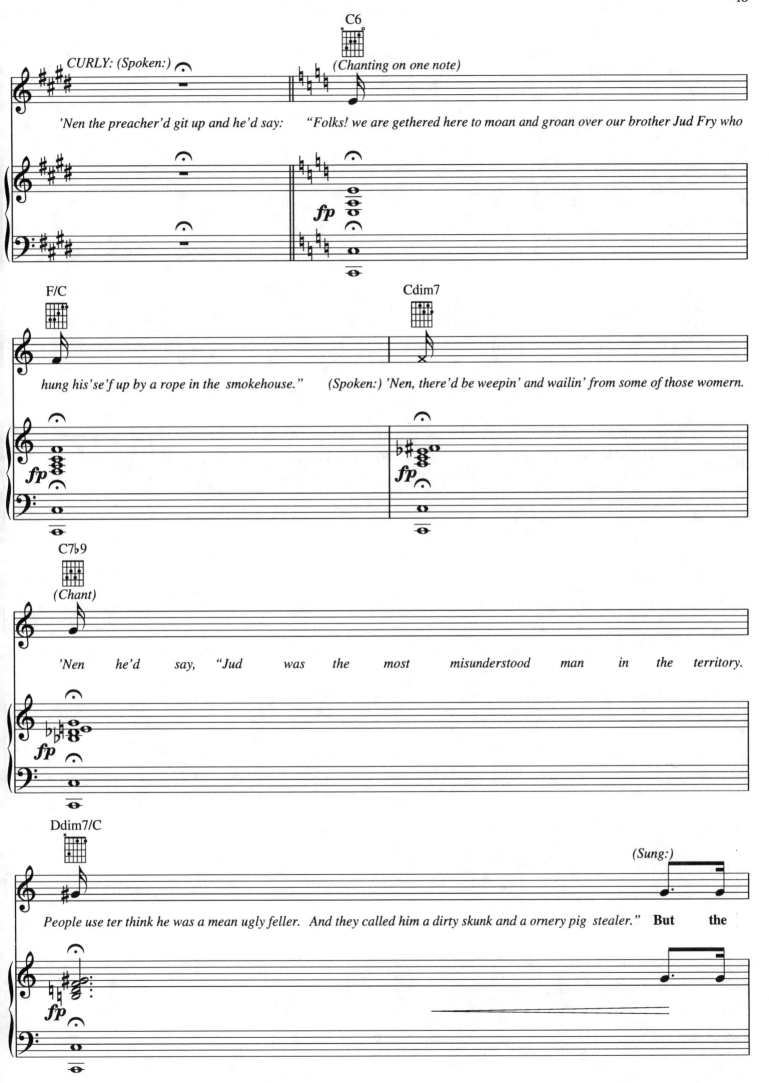

LONELY ROOM

Lyrics by OSCAR HAMMERSTEIN II
Music by RICHARD RODGERS

THE FARMER AND THE COWMAN

Lyrics by OSCAR HAMMERSTEIN II
Music by RICHARD RODGERS

OUT OF MY DREAMS

Lyrics by OSCAR HAMMERSTEIN II
Music by RICHARD RODGERS

ALL ER NOTHIN'

Lyrics by OSCAR HAMMERSTEIN II
Music by RICHARD RODGERS

WILL: You'll have to be a lit-tle more stand-off-ish when fel-lers of-fer you a bug-gy ride._____ ANNIE: I'll

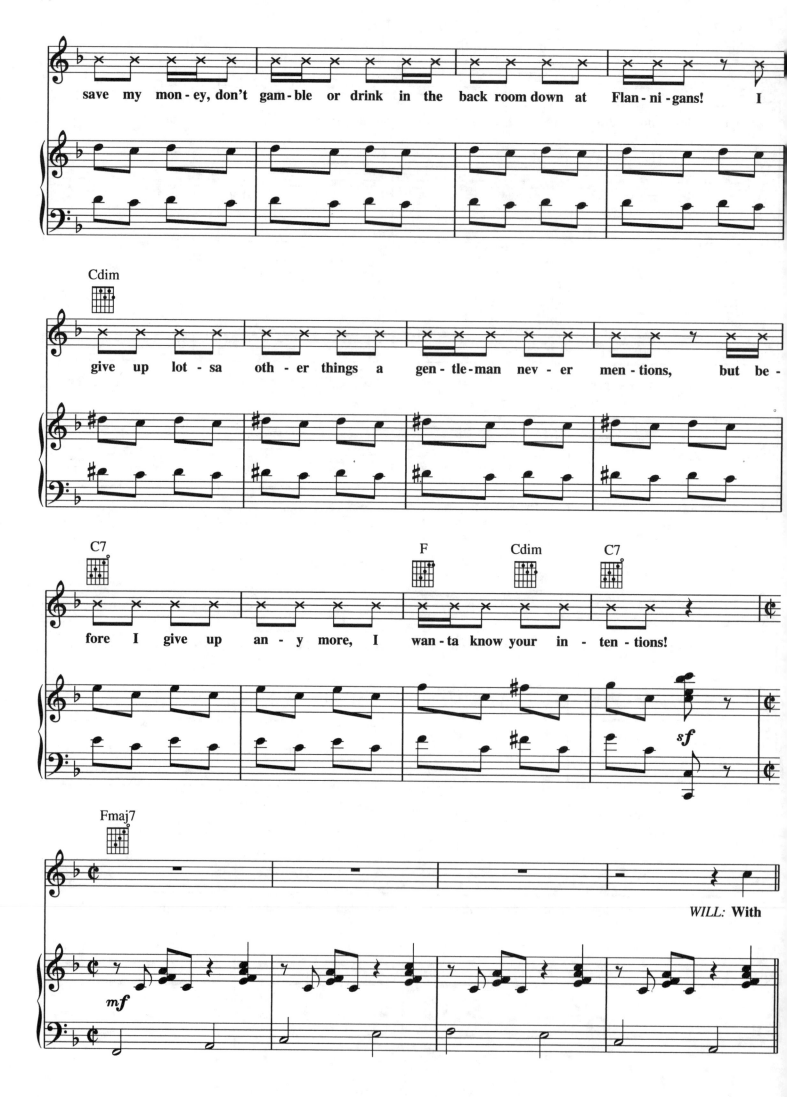

OKLAHOMA

Lyrics by OSCAR HAMMERSTEIN II
Music by RICHARD RODGERS